WILD HABITATS
of the British Isles

Hedgerows

Louise and Richard Spilsbury

Heinemann
LIBRARY

www.heinemann.co.uk/library

Visit our website to find out more information about **Heinemann Library** books.

To order:

☎ Phone 44 (0) 1865 888066

▤ Send a fax to 44 (0) 1865 314091

▢ Visit the Heinemann Bookshop at www.heinemann.co.uk/library to browse our catalogue and order online.

First published in Great Britain by Heinemann Library, Halley Court, Jordan Hill, Oxford OX2 8EJ, part of Harcourt Education.

Heinemann is a registered trademark of Harcourt Education Ltd.

Editorial: Lucy Thunder and Helen Cannons
Design: David Poole and Kamae Design
Picture Research: Hannah Taylor and Liz Savery
Production: Edward Moore

Originated by P.T. Repro Multi-Warna
Printed in China by WKT Company Limited

The paper used to print this book comes from sustainable resources.

ISBN 0 431 12124 9
08 07 06 05 04
10 9 8 7 6 5 4 3 2 1

British Library Cataloguing in Publication Data
Spilsbury, Louise and Spilsbury, Richard
Hedgerows. − (Wild habitats of the British Isles)
577.5'55'0941
A full catalogue record for this book is available from the British Library.

Acknowledgements

The Publishers would like to thank the following for permission to reproduce photographs: Al Anderson p**24**; Andy Purcell p**25**; FLPA/D T Grewcock p**29**; FLPA/David Hosking p**22**; FLPA/J Watkins p**19**; FLPA/Jeremy Early p**9**; FLPA/M B Withers p**16**; FLPA/Robert Canis p**18**; Jason Hawkes Aerial Photography Library p**28**; Jo Pitson p**20**; Nature Picture Library/Dietmar Nill p**17**; NHPA/Alan Barnes p**12**; NHPA/E A Janes p**6**; NHPA/Jane Gifford p**4**; NHPA/Stephen Dalton p**27** bottom; Ordnance Survey pp**10** top, **20** top, **24** top; Oxford Scientific Films p**14**; Oxford Scientific Films/Terry Heathcote p**15**; Peter Evans pp**10** bottom, **23** top, **23** bottom; Photodisc pp**27** top, **5** top; Tudor Photography p**7**; Woodfall Wild Images pp**8**, **11**; Woodfall Wild Images/Bob Gibbons p**13**; Woodfall Wild Images/David Woodfall pp**5** bottom, **26**; Woodfall Wild Images/John Robinson p**21** top.

Cover photograph of a flowering roadside hedgerow, reproduced with permission of NHPA/David Woodfall.

The Publishers would like to thank Michael Scott, wildlife consultant and writer, for his assistance in the preparation of this book.

Every effort has been made to contact copyright holders of any material reproduced in this book. Any omissions will be rectified in subsequent printings if notice is given to the Publishers.

Disclaimer

All the Internet addresses (URLs) given in this book were valid at the time of going to press. However, due to the dynamic nature of the Internet, some addresses may have changed, or sites may have changed or ceased to exist since publication. While the author and Publishers regret any inconvenience this may cause readers, no responsibility for any such changes can be accepted by either the author or the Publishers.

Contents

Hedgerow habitats 4

Types of hedgerows 6

Plants in a hedgerow 8

CASE STUDY: Bridgend, Wales 10

Hedgerow mini-beasts 12

Toads and snakes 14

Birds of the hedgerow 16

Hedgerow mammals 18

CASE STUDY: South Devon, England 20

Seasonal hedgerows 22

CASE STUDY: Meikleour, Scotland 24

Hedgerows under threat 26

Protecting hedgerows 28

Glossary 30

Find out more 31

Index 32

Any words appearing in the text in bold, **like this**, are explained in the Glossary.

Hedgerow habitats

Hedges are rows of trees or bushes planted by people to mark boundaries between areas of land. Hedgerows are found all over the British Isles. Most hedges divide up farmland into fields. They were originally planted for several reasons, such as to stop **livestock** escaping from a field or to stop people or animals damaging **crops**.

Hedges can also be found bordering churchyards, parks and gardens, areas of houses, lanes and roads. Landowners often planted these hedges to show other people which bits of land they owned, or to show others where they should not go.

A hedgerow is usually a row of thick bushes, trees or a mixture of both. These **woody** plants are tough enough to make a strong barrier. Some hedges are planted on top of tall soil banks and these form especially high boundaries.

Get this!

There are about 450,000 kilometres (280,000 miles) of hedgerow in Britain – that's enough hedgerow to circle the Earth twelve times!

↑ Many of the hedgerows of the British Isles divide farmland into a patchwork of fields.

What is a hedgerow habitat?

A **habitat** is the natural home of a group of organisms (living things). Their habitat provides them with what they need to survive, such as sources of **nutrients** and shelter from bad weather or **predators**. Hedgerows are an important British habitat. The animals and plants in a hedge are interdependent – their lives are closely related. For example, blackbirds may nest in a hedgerow, sheltered amongst thorny brambles. When the birds eat blackberries they spread the seeds through their droppings, and new brambles may grow.

Each hedgerow is different partly because of where it grows. For example, some hedgerows near the coast of the British Isles are made of gorse. This plant can more easily grow in the **exposed** conditions near the sea than can, for example, a beech tree. Hedges next to woods often contain woodland plant **species**, such as bluebells.

↑ Animals, such as foxes, find food and shelter in hedgerows.

Hedgerows offer a range of mini-habitats within one habitat. On the outside, they are exposed to sunlight, rain and wind. The sheltered interior of a hedge may be shadier, cooler and drier. The base of a hedge is shady and damp. Different hedgerow organisms prefer to live in different parts of a hedge. This picture shows the mini-habitats of a hedge, from the flowery base up to the tree, where birds can perch.

Types of hedgerows

British hedges can be roughly divided into three types, depending on how old they are. The age of a hedge is important, because in general the older the hedge, the more **species** live there.

Ancient hedges

The first people who lived in the British Isles did not farm. They hunted wild animals and gathered plants to eat from the forests that covered the land. Farming – keeping **livestock** and growing plants in fields – began around 8000 years ago. People cleared vast areas of forest to make farmland. They often left strips of woodland to form hedges around their fields. Some of these ancient hedgerows still survive today. The kinds of plants that grow in them, such as hazel and bluebell, are **native** species. They have grown in the British Isles for thousands of years.

↑ Lines of hawthorn bushes form dense, thorny barriers that large animals, such as cows and sheep, cannot get through.

Hazel

Hazel is a quick-growing tree. It makes two different types of flowers in spring – a small female flower and a long male flower, usually called a catkin. When wind blows **pollen** from the catkin on to the female flower, it starts to grow into a hazelnut. Hazelnuts are important food for hedgerow animals, such as mice.

Enclosures and hedgerows

About 300 years ago, laws were passed in Britain that increased hedgerows dramatically. These laws – called Enclosure Acts – resulted in changes in field size and who owned them. This meant landowners planted quick-growing hedges around the new fields. The Enclosure Acts helped some landowners become rich, because bigger fields could be used to grow more **crops** or contain more livestock. However, it also made poor people poorer, by enclosing lots of common land that previously everyone had been able to use.

Enclosure hedgerows are often straight and edge large, square fields. Usually fewer species live in these hedges than in ancient hedgerows. However, they are still important and rich **habitats** for wildlife.

Modern hedgerows

New hedgerows are still planted today. They are usually made up of one species, such as privet, holly or beech. In general, if there are fewer plant species in a hedge, there is less food and shelter for fewer animals.

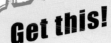

Get this!

Scientists have uncovered the remains of a hedge that was planted around 40 BC, when Romans occupied Britain. This is the earliest evidence of a hedge ever found in Britain.

← When houses are closely packed together, hedges can make gardens separate and private spaces.

Plants in a hedgerow

The variety of plant **species** that grows in a hedgerow depends partly on what was planted when the hedge was first built. It also depends on what plants have sprung up there naturally over the years. Many seeds blow into a hedge or are dropped there by animals. Some will **germinate** if conditions are right and become part of the hedge. Trees and shrubs, such as ash and elder, in a hedgerow will have usually established themselves there naturally.

Get this!

Be a hedge detective! Choose a 30-metre length of hedgerow and count the number of tree and shrub species in it. Multiply the number of species by 100. The answer is the rough age of the hedge!

Hedge levels

Plants grow at different levels within a hedge. This is because growing conditions, such as light and moisture, vary. The base of a hedge is usually shady and moist. This is especially the case on the northern side, which in the British Isles is out of direct sunlight for much of the year. Some hedges have a water-filled ditch along their base, making conditions even wetter. The tangle of moist undergrowth at a hedge base may include grasses, stinging nettles, violets and ferns. A common fern in hedges is the hart's tongue fern, which gets its name from its long **fronds**. They are shaped a little like the tongue of a deer (or hart). Ferns need moist conditions to **reproduce** properly.

Wild garlic and bluebells have emerged from bulbs in the sheltered soil beneath a hedge. ➔

Hedge scaffolding

The heart of any hedge is its trees and shrubs. Apart from creating a barrier, these strong plants also form a 'scaffolding' through which other plants grow. Taller plants, such as foxglove, grow through the hedge base. Foxgloves are tall enough to display their spikes of pink flowers above other plants, where they are easily seen by insect **pollinators**.

Other tall plants produce flat, open umbrella-shaped groups of flowers. These act as flowery landing pads where visiting flies and beetles can sip **nectar**.

↑ Each flower head on a cow parsley plant is up to 6 centimetres across. The umbrella-like flower heads are made up of hundreds of individual flowers.

Climbing plants

When you are walking along a hedge, you will notice that some plants grow up in the hedge without the support of strong stems. Ivy is a woody **climber** with shiny dark green leaves. It attaches itself as it climbs using little sticky roots that grip the bark of trees. A plant called old man's beard climbs around the top of hedges by twisting curly **tendrils** around the stems and branches of other hedge plants. It gets its name from its fluffy seed cases that look rather like clumps of white hair.

Bridgend, Wales

In 1999, scientists carried out a special survey of hedgerows in the area of Bridgend, South Wales. They selected 30-metre lengths of particular hedges. They then recorded which **species** grew there. This showed that most Bridgend hedges are full of species with, on average, eight types of woody plant in each one. This suggests the hedges were planted a long time ago. The scientists also discovered that the wider the hedge, especially at the base, the more plant species that live there.

Thorns

The commonest woody species found at Bridgend were hawthorn and blackthorn. Hawthorn is often called may because May is the month in which it flowers. Many beetles and flies **pollinate** the hawthorn's small pink and white flowers, attracted to their sweet scent. By autumn, the **fertilized** flowers have developed into small red fruit called haws. Many birds and **mammals** eat haws. Blackthorn grows flowers even earlier. Its white flowers stand out against its black branches. Blackthorn fruit are shiny, purple-black sloes (like plums).

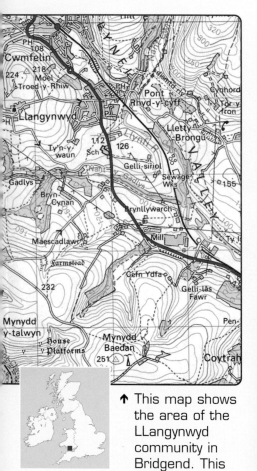

↑ This map shows the area of the LLangynwyd community in Bridgend. This is one of the areas that took part in the hedgerow survey.

In summer, foxgloves and bracken grow tall through the base of this Bridgend hedge. →

Rich in species

The hedgerows in Bridgend contain a rich mixture of plants. **Native** trees include elm, hazel, ash, holly and oak. There are also **introduced** tree species, such as horse chestnut and sycamore, that come from outside Britain. Sycamore was widely planted by people in the British Isles in the 18th century because they liked the way it looked. Sycamores are quick to grow naturally from seed in gaps in hedges. In general, fewer animal species live on sycamore than on native plant species, such as hawthorn and oak.

Get this!

Of the 49,000 kilometres (30,447 miles) of hedges in Wales, nearly half are ancient hedgerows rich in different species.

← Dog rose is the commonest climbing plant in Bridgend hedgerows. It bears pink flowers in early summer and red fruit called hips in autumn. The hips contain lots of tiny sticky seeds, used by children in the past as itching powder!

Oak markers

Oak trees grow in around a third of the Bridgend hedges that were surveyed. Oaks have **lobed** leaves, greyish bark and fruit called acorns. In the Middle Ages, oak trees were often planted as markers in hedgerows to show where strips of field belonging to different people met. Some hedges today still have oak trees spaced out along their length.

Hedgerow mini-beasts

Hedgerows are an important **habitat** for mini-beasts, such as **insects**, spiders and snails. The plants in hedges provide shelter from **predators** and bad weather. They also supply a wide range of foods, including flower **nectar** and leaves. **Carnivorous** (flesh-eating) mini-beasts feed on some of the **herbivores** that eat the plants.

Insects

There are around 1500 **species** of insect in different hedges around the British Isles. Many beetles lay their eggs in and feed on rotting wood at the base of hedges or under tree bark. Grasshoppers use their long back legs to leap from plant to plant looking for leaves to eat. Aphids and shield bugs stick their long tube mouths into soft plant stems to feed on the **sap** inside.

If you see hoverflies by a hedgerow you may mistake them for wasps or bees. Many hoverflies have yellow and black stripes to frighten off predators, even though they do not have stings like wasps and bees! Hoverflies are so-named because they **hover** over hedgerow plants to find nectar or somewhere to lay their eggs.

↑ The pearl-bordered fritillary is a rare butterfly. It lays its eggs on violets at the base of some hedgerows in the British Isles.

12

Spiders

Spiders produce silk strands that they usually use to spin sticky webs to catch their **prey**. Most spiders in British hedges are small, usually around 2 millimetres across, and very light. They move quickly from plant to plant or between hedges to find food. Spiders move between plants and hedges by spinning silk strands that carry them in the wind.

The four-spot orb weaver is the largest British hedgerow spider. Its body is nearly 2 centimetres long. Orb weavers spin a wheel-shaped web between plant stems or branches. They catch mostly jumping insects, such as grasshoppers and crickets. Orb web females, like many other spider species, are much bigger than males. The male approaches the female very carefully when it is time to **mate**. Otherwise he may become another one of her meals!

↑ It is easier to see delicate money spider webs when they are covered in morning dew.

Slugs and snails

Slugs and snails make slime so they can slide over rough surfaces more easily. Slugs prefer the damper, shaded spaces at hedge bases. Snails, such as the banded snail, can survive **exposed** conditions on the outsides of hedges because, unlike slugs, they have waterproof, protective shells to retreat into.

Toads and snakes

Toads are **amphibians** – animals with smooth, slimy skin that lay their eggs in wet places. The ditches alongside many hedgerows provide homes for toads. These ditches were originally dug to drain water from land or to help mark boundaries.

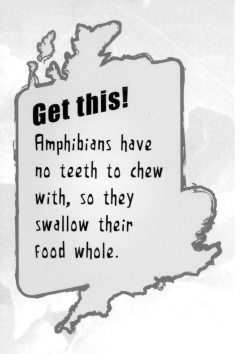

Get this!

Amphibians have no teeth to chew with, so they swallow their food whole.

From egg to adult

Toads have knobbly skin and short back legs. They lay strings of soft eggs, called spawn, in ditches. After a few weeks, babies called tadpoles wriggle free from the spawn. Tadpoles are more like little fish than their parents. They have no legs, long tails and breathe underwater using **gills**. They feed on tiny animals and plants in the water.

As they grow, tadpoles change bit by bit. Their legs grow, their tail gets shorter and they start to breathe using lungs. The young toads finally leave the water to start hunting **prey** on land. They use their sticky tongues to catch **insects** and slugs around the bases of hedgerows.

↑ A toad can flick its sticky tongue out and back into its mouth again, to catch prey, such as a fly, in one-tenth of a second!

British snakes

Snakes are reptiles, animals with scaly skin that lay their eggs on land. There are two species of snake in and around hedgerows in the British Isles – grass snakes and adders. Both **hibernate** through cold winters in burrows or under logs. They may come out on warm winter days, but they only fully emerge again in spring.

All snakes are **carnivores**. They search for prey by flicking their forked tongue in the air. The tongue catches tiny scents from small animals, such as mice. Grass snakes are dark green snakes with a yellow or orange collar-like mark on their neck. They search ditches for tadpoles and toads and they climb hedgerows hunting for insects. To feed, adders slither amongst the plants low down in a hedge hunting for voles, mice and toads. They kill their prey using a poisonous bite.

↑ Snakes can also climb to find food. This grass snake is climbing up the roots of a tree in the New Forest.

Adder skins

You may sometimes find an old snake skin among hedgerows. It may have belonged to an adder. Adders are grey or brown snakes with a zigzag pattern on their back. They shed their skin after winter hibernation. The old, damaged skin is replaced by a new one that grows underneath. Adders rub off the old skin against plants in drier parts of hedgerows.

Birds of the hedgerow

Hedgerows attract different types of birds. Hedgerows provide sheltered nesting sites and nest materials such as twigs. They also provide a rich supply of food both for adult birds and their chicks.

Hedge nesters

Hedgerow birds, such as yellowhammers, make new nests each spring. Male yellowhammers are small birds with a striking mustard-coloured head and chest. A female yellowhammer is less brightly coloured. She builds a nest out of grasses and moss low down in hawthorn hedges. She lines it with fine grass or animal hair found on fences. Yellowhammers lay up to six white eggs. The chicks hatch within two weeks and are fed small **insects** and seeds by their parents. It only takes two weeks until the chicks are ready to fly off.

Dunnocks and cuckoos

Dunnocks (shown here) are small grey and brown hedge-nesting birds. Cuckoos are larger striped birds that have a special way of rearing their young – they get another bird to do it! Cuckoos often sneak into a dunnock nest and lay a single, similar-looking egg amongst the blue dunnock eggs. When the cuckoo chick hatches, it pushes out any dunnock eggs or chicks. The adult dunnocks then feed the cuckoo chick until it is ready to fly away.

Hedgerow food

Hedgerow plants provide food for both insect-eating and seeds or berry-eating birds. In spring and summer many insects come to feed on hedgerow flowers along with spiders and other **invertebrates**. In autumn, birds feed on seeds, nuts and berries from hedge plants. Hedges also provide shelter from weather and predators while birds eat.

Song thrushes are medium-sized brown birds with a white speckled front. Their clear song sounds a bit like a flute playing. Song thrushes eat worms, slugs and snails at the bases of hedges. Blackcaps are small birds with black feathers on their head. During summer, they use their thin beaks to snatch spiders and caterpillars from hedgerow plants, but during winter, they eat berries.

Bird predators

Many bird **predators** look for food in hedges. Sparrowhawks are **birds of prey**, specially **adapted** to hunting. They have excellent eyesight, sharp claws and a hooked beak to find and kill **prey**. Sparrowhawks often catch thrushes and finches. Magpies and crows are less fussy about what they eat. They eat anything from animals killed on roads to worms, fruit and seeds.

Song thrushes crack open snail shells on stones to get at the soft flesh inside. ↓

Hedgerow mammals

Hedgerows form important sheltered pathways between areas of woodland. Small hedgerow **mammals**, such as voles, mice and shrews, use the cover provided by hedges to remain out of sight of **predators** such as **birds of prey**. The cover provided by hedgerows is especially useful when they are rearing their young or looking for food.

Field mice use their good balance to reach food such as nuts and hips in hedgerows. ↓

Young mammals

Field voles often dig underground tunnels in the dry soil of hedge banks. They make grass nests in the tunnels where they give birth to young. Newborn voles have no hair and their eyes are closed. As they get bigger, their eyes open and they grow hair. The babies feed on milk from their mother at first. Gradually they start to eat grass, seeds, **insects** and **fungi** brought to them by their mother. Eventually they start to make feeding trips with her.

Shrew caravan

Baby shrews stick close to their mother when she is out hunting invertebrates at the base of a hedge. They form a shrew caravan. One baby grips its mother's tail with its teeth, the next baby grips the first one's tail and so on. Then they move off!

Nibbled hazelnuts

When field mice nibble hard hazelnuts beneath a hedge they leave rough-edged holes to get to the food inside (like the nut below). Dormice nibble smooth holes (like the nut above).

Hares

Adult brown hares are around twice the size of rabbits. They have black-tipped ears. Female hares often give birth in the long grass bordering hedges. Their babies – called leverets – are born with fur and able to run. The female feeds them milk once each night. For the rest of the time she leaves them alone. The leverets huddle together and lie still in a hollow in the grass or a dip in the soil known as a form. This keeps the leverets out of sight of predators until the female returns.

Night-time visitors

Many mammals are **nocturnal** – they are active at night. Nocturnal predators include hedgehogs, owls, badgers and foxes. Hedgehogs rest during the day and hunt along hedges at night. They use their senses of smell and hearing to find slugs, snails, insects and worms to eat. Hedgehogs try to put off **predators** using their sharp spines. Spines are special hard hairs that hedgehogs have all over their backs. Hedgehogs can curl up into a tight prickly ball, tucking in their head and feet until danger has passed.

Hedgehogs use their sharp teeth to pierce and crush their food.
↓

South Devon, England

Devon has more hedgerows than any other county in the British Isles. Many of its hedges grow on tall soil banks, their sides covered with grasses and other plants. Often the hedges border lanes.

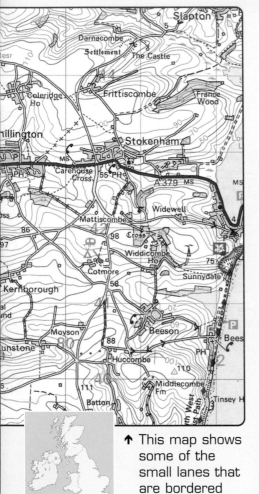

↑ This map shows some of the small lanes that are bordered with hedges in South Devon.

Dense plants close in many Devon lanes, making them very narrow and shady. ➔

Life in honeysuckle

Honeysuckle is a typical **climber** on hedges along Devon lanes. Young honeysuckle stems are soft and green and twine around other plants. As they get older, the stems become woody and tough, and covered in flaky bark. Honeysuckle flowers are curved yellow or white tubes with **nectar** that smells like honey. Honeysuckle is an important food plant for different animals including bugs and caterpillars. Tangled honeysuckle stems also provide shelter for small animals.

Dormice are small orange-yellow **mammals** with a thick bushy tail. They live in some overgrown Devon hedges. Dormice usually spend the daytime in nests they make from shredded honeysuckle bark surrounded with leaves. They clamber through the hedge at night, searching for a range of food including honeysuckle **pollen**, nectar, nuts and berries.

Flying insect-eaters

Insects flying along Devon hedges attract a variety of **predators**. Some insects, such as grasshoppers, take to the air during the day. Birds, such as swallows, fly low along hedgerows catching them. Other **nocturnal** insects, such as moths, fly at dusk and during the night. This is also when bats go hunting.

Bats are the only mammals that can fly. Their wings are made of leathery skin stretched tight between very long finger bones. Bats hunt their **prey** in the dark. They make very high squeaks and listen for echoes using large, sensitive ears. The sounds echo when they bounce off something, such as a flying insect. The lesser horseshoe bat is one of the smallest bat species in Devon.

Horseshoe bats get their name from the distinctive shape of their nose! ↓

Elephant hawkmoths

Elephant hawkmoths get their name from their caterpillars (a moth begins life as a caterpillar). These are brownish grey with little folds down their length and look like mini elephant trunks! Elephant hawkmoths are around 5 centimetres across with a pinkish green body and wings. They fly around honeysuckle flowers, like these, at dusk when its perfume smells strongest. They reach the sweet nectar, deep inside the flowers, by uncoiling their long tube-shaped mouth.

Seasonal hedgerows

Hedgerows look different through the year. Different plant **species** produce leaves, flowers and fruit at different times of year as the seasons change. Different animal species live in and around a hedge as the amount of shelter and food changes.

New growth

In winter, the weather is usually cold and wet. Most hedgerow trees and shrubs have bare branches and there are very few flowers around. Only a few **evergreen** plants, such as ivy and holly, still have leaves. In spring, when the weather is getting warmer, hedgerows start to get greener. New leaves or flowers emerge from buds at the tips of tree branches. Plants, such as snowdrops and bluebells, grow from underground bulbs. Their flowers attract **insect pollinators**, such as bumblebees. Bumblebees spend winter in underground nests. They can remain active in the cool spring air as they are covered in fur that helps keep their bodies warm.

Deciduous plants

Most British hedgerow trees and shrubs are **deciduous**. They drop all their leaves in autumn and grow new ones in spring. If their soft, tender leaves stayed on branches over winter, they would be damaged by the cold. In winter, most shrub and tree branches in hedges are bare. However, hedgerows provide vital shelter for animals against bad weather.

Spring and summer

In the warmth of late spring and summer, different plants emerge from seeds and roots sheltered in hedge bases. Fern **fronds** are tightly rolled up when they first appear and gradually unwind. **Invertebrates**, such as beetles, slugs and moths, hatch from underground eggs or **pupae**. Birds sing to attract other birds to **mate** with. They start work building nests and raising their young amongst the dense leaves of hedgerow plants.

Autumn and winter

As summer turns to autumn, plant fruits ripen. Animals feast on the rich supply of oily nuts and seeds and sweet fruit. Many uneaten seeds fall to ground where they remain until they sprout in the following spring. Fallen leaves, dead wood and other plant remains form a layer called **leaf litter** at the base of hedgerows in autumn. **Fungi**, such as mushrooms and toadstools, grow among the leaf litter and help to rot it down. The fungi use some of the **nutrients** to grow but leave some in the soil. These nutrients help other new plants to grow in spring.

↑ Fern fronds unfurl in spring and summer.

A food web diagram shows what eats what in a **habitat**. This is a food web for a hedgerow in summer. ↓

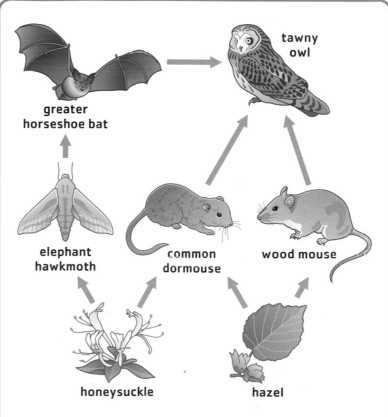

tawny owl

greater horseshoe bat

elephant hawkmoth

common dormouse

wood mouse

honeysuckle

hazel

not to scale

23

Meikleour, Scotland

The Meikleour hedge was planted in 1746 as a boundary to mark the Marquess of Lansdowne's estate in Perthshire, Scotland. The hedge is made up of two 500-metre-long rows of beech trees. Each tree is around 30 metres tall!

↑ This shows the location of the Meikleour hedge in the centre of the map, highlighted in dark blue.

Beech trees

Beech hedges are **deciduous** but remain shady places all year around. This is partly because with regular cutting many small branches grow from the trunks, forming thick undergrowth. The **leaf litter** beneath a beech hedge is slow to rot. This is because the beech leaves are rich in a tough chemical called tannin. Few other plants thrive in the shady, low-**nutrient** soil but there are many **fungi**.

Bird's-nest orchid

The bird's-nest orchid is sometimes found growing in beech leaf litter in the British Isles. The orchid is white or pale yellow and its roots form a tangled ball that looks a bit like a nest. This unusual plant does not make its own food by **photosynthesis**. Instead, it absorbs all its food through its roots from the fungi that live in the leaf litter.

← The Meikleour hedge is probably the most famous hedge in the British Isles. It takes a team of four gardeners about six weeks to trim it, every few years.

Life among beech trees

Although beech trees are not **native** to northern Britain, they attract a wide range of animals, especially in autumn. This is when the trees produce their nuts. Beech fruit are spiky cases that protect two or three nuts until they are ripe. The nuts, called mast, contain a lot of fat. **Mammals**, such as badgers, and birds, such as chaffinches, seek out mast to eat. This helps them fatten up before the cold of winter sets in. Squirrels store beech mast in holes in trees or under the ground. In winter they remember roughly where they buried them, and then use their good sense of smell to pinpoint the location of the mast.

Grey squirrels

Grey squirrels were introduced to the British Isles from North America over 100 years ago. They are now much more common than the native red squirrel. At Meikleour, grey squirrels live in the beech trees and feed on beech mast using their long, sharp front teeth. They also strip off the hard outer bark of beech trees to eat the soft bark beneath. Grey squirrels make nests, called dreys, out of beech branches and leaves. They shelter in their dreys, and rear their young in them.

Hedgerows under threat

The hedgerows of the British Isles are under threat. The main reasons for this is that people have changed the way they use and care for farmland.

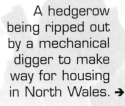

Unwanted hedges

Many hedges were removed between the 1940s and the end of the 20th century as some farmers made larger fields to grow more **crops**. Other hedges were removed because some farmers no longer needed them to keep **livestock** in fields, or because fences were cheaper and easier to look after. Many farmers keep their crops free of **weeds** and **insect pests** by spraying chemicals on them. Some removed hedges because they believed these weeds and pests grew or sheltered there.

Many other hedges were destroyed to clear land for housing. New roads were built and existing roads made wider. This is because more and more people in Britain rely on vehicles to get around and to transport food and other things.

A hedgerow being ripped out by a mechanical digger to make way for housing in North Wales. →

Hedge care

Many hedges are trimmed today using machines. This is much quicker and cheaper than doing it by hand, but can damage hedgerow plants. Over time it may kill off side branches, making hedges tall and thin. If hedges are trimmed too often or at the wrong time of year, other wildlife can suffer. For example, nesting hedgerow birds and their chicks risk being **exposed** to bad weather or **predators**.

Road dangers

Wildlife in hedges bordering roads face other problems. Exhaust fumes **pollute** the air and dropped litter pollutes the ground. Small **mammals** such as voles may become trapped inside discarded bottles and eventually starve to death. Many animals moving between hedges on either side of a road also risk being run over.

↑ Dog rose hips, like these, can be an important food source for wildlife. When hedges are trimmed at the wrong time of year, it can destroy the hips.

Dormice under threat

Experts say that dormice have vanished from two-thirds of the hedgerows in which they were living twenty years ago. One of the reasons dormice have become rare in the British Isles is because hedgerows are cut back by machines every year. This severe trimming cuts away plant growth that would produce the berries and nuts dormice need to survive winter **hibernation**.

Protecting hedgerows

Most people today understand the importance of protecting hedgerows. You are much more likely to see a new hedge being planted than one being removed. There are many different reasons why hedges are now protected.

Hedgerows as habitats

Hedgerows are vital places for wildlife to live, feed and travel along. Many rare **species**, such as dormice, thrive in hedgerows. As the area of woodland in the British Isles has decreased, hedgerows have become the main remaining **habitat** for many woodland species. Hedges are also important because they are pieces of history. If you look around the British countryside, there are plenty of hedges even older than ancient castles or churches. Hedges also make the countryside look more interesting and attractive.

Protecting topsoil

Hedges help stop topsoil erosion. This is when winds blow or rain washes the top layer of soil away from the ground. Topsoil is important for farmers, as it is full of **nutrients** that help **crops** grow. Hedges form barriers against strong winds and rain, but also stop the eroded soil being lost from fields.

↑ For many years, hedgerows were removed to make field sizes larger. This is now illegal.

Farmers and hedgerows

Many farmers protect hedgerows, partly because they are so useful. Hedgerows provide effective field boundaries, hold in **livestock** and provide it with shelter from bad weather. Hedgerows are also cheaper to make and to maintain than stone walls. One of the things farmers do to care for hedges is avoid spraying chemicals on the strips of land nearest hedges. This prevents wildflowers being harmed. Hedges also provide shelter for helpful **predators,** such as lacewings, that eat crop **pests**.

How do people care for hedgerows?

Hedgerows in the British Isles have been protected by law since 1997. It is illegal to remove hedges without permission. **Conservation** organizations, such as the National Trust, encourage landowners to look after and restore old or overgrown hedges using traditional methods, such as hedgelaying. Hedgelaying is when overgrown shrub and tree stems are cut almost all the way through in winter, and laid down almost flat. New shoots grow from the stems and form a healthy bushy hedge.

← Groups, such as the British Trust for Conservation Volunteers, organize hedgelaying courses where interested people take part in hedge restoration.

Glossary

adapted when a living thing has special features that help it survive in a habitat

amphibian group of egg-laying animals with moist skin that usually lives in water when young and on land when adult

bird of prey bird that hunts animals for food

carnivore flesh-eating animal

climber type of plant that clings or twists around others to get taller

conservation taking action to protect plants, animals and wild habitats

crop useful food plant grown by people

deciduous describes plants that lose all their leaves by winter and grow new ones in spring

evergreen not deciduous

exposed open to strong winds, rain and cold

fertilize in flowering plants, when pollen from a male combines with an egg from a female to form seeds

frond leaf of certain plants such as ferns and seaweed

fungi organism such as a mushroom that usually rots (breaks down) plants to absorb nutrients

germinate when a new plant grows roots and shoots as it emerges from a seed

gills special body parts used by some animals, such as fish, to breathe underwater

habitat type of place where a plant or animal lives

herbivore animal that eats only plants

hibernation deep sleep during cold weather

hover controlled flight when it is possible to stay in one place in the air

insect six-legged animal which, when adult, has three body sections: head, thorax (chest) and abdomen (stomach)

introduced non-native organism that lives in a country because it was brought there

invertebrate animal without a backbone, such as a worm or insect

leaf litter layer of dead and decaying leaves on woodland floor or beneath a hedge

livestock farm animals such as cows kept for useful products such as milk

lobed with several curves along its edges

mammal type of animal with some hair. Female mammals can give birth to live young, which they feed on their own milk.

mate what a male and female animal do to make new offspring (young)

native living naturally in a particular place

nectar sweet liquid made by some flowering plants to attract animal pollinators

nocturnal active at night

nutrients chemicals that nourish organisms

pest nuisance or damaging animal

photosynthesis how plants make their own food using water, carbon dioxide (a gas in air) and energy from sunlight

pollen small protein-rich grains in a flower

pollination when pollen travels from the male part of one flower to the female part of another flower to form seeds

pollution when chemicals or waste escapes into the air, water or soil and damages the habitat there for plants and animals

predator animal that catches and eats other animals

prey animal caught by predators to eat

pupa a special case formed by many insects, in which they change from young to adult

reproduce to breed or produce young

sap sugary fluid inside a plant stem

species group of living things that are similar in many ways and can breed together

tendril special thin leaf used by climbers to twist around other plants

weed type of plant that is usually unwanted

woody plant with hard, strong stems

Find out more

Books

British Plants, Angela Royston (Heinemann, 1999)

Collins Field Guide: Birds of Britain and Europe, Roger Tory Peterson, Guy Mountfort, P.A.D. Hollom (Collins Field Guides, 1993)

Collins Field Guide: Insects of Britain and Northern Europe, Michael Chinery (Collins Field Guides, 1993)

Websites

The British Trust for Conservation Volunteers has a website with information about how people can help to conserve British habitats: www.btcv.org

The Wildlife Trust has a website with information about plants and animals that live in hedgerows and how to manage hedgerows for wildlife: www.wildlifetrusts.org

The Scottish Wildlife Trust has a special habitat sheet called 'What are hedgerows?' at: www.swt.org.uk

The Environment Agency is a government organization that helps protect different habitats in the UK. They have lots of information about wildlife habitats in England and Wales on their website: www.environment-agency.gov.uk

Index

adders 15
age of a hedge 8
ancient hedgerows 6, 7, 11

bats 21
beech trees 5, 24, 25
birds 5, 10, 16–17, 21, 23, 25, 27
bird's nest orchid 24
birds of prey 17, 18
blackthorn 10
Bridgend, Wales 10–11
bumblebees 22
butterflies 12

climbing plants 9, 20
conservation 29
cuckoos 16

deciduous plants 22, 24
Devon 20-1
ditches 8, 14, 15
dog rose 11
dormice 18, 20, 23, 27, 28
dunnocks 16

Enclosure Acts 7
enclosure hedgerows 7

farming 4, 6, 7, 26, 28, 29
ferns 8, 23
flowers 5, 6, 10, 11, 20, 22, 24

food web 23
fruit, nuts and seeds 5, 10, 11, 17, 23, 25, 27
fungi 23, 24

gorse 5

habitats and mini-habitats 5, 7, 28
hares 19
hawthorn 6, 10
hazel 6
hedge bases 5, 8, 13, 23
hedge destruction 26
hedge levels 8
hedge trimming 27
hedgehogs 19
hedgelaying 29
honeysuckle 20
hoverflies 12

insects 10, 12, 14, 17, 18, 19, 21, 22, 23, 29

leaf litter 23, 24
livestock 4, 6, 7, 26, 29

mammals 10, 18-19, 20, 21, 25, 27
mast 25
Meikleour, Scotland 24, 25
mice 6, 15, 18, 20, 27, 28
modern hedgerows 7
moths 21, 23

nutrients 5, 23, 28

oak trees 11

plant species 5, 6, 7, 8–9, 10, 11, 20, 22, 23
predators 5, 12, 14, 15, 17, 18, 19, 21, 27, 29

'scaffolding' plants 9
seasonal changes 22–3
shelter 5, 12, 17, 20, 29
shrews 18
slugs and snails 13, 14, 17, 19, 23
snakes 15
spiders 13, 17
squirrels 25
sycamore 11

threats to hedgerows 26–7
thrushes 17
toads 14, 15
topsoil erosion 28
tree species 8, 11, 22, 24, 25

voles 15, 18, 27

yellowhammers 16